GU00976172

# PREPARE
## THE WAY
### OF THE
# LORD

Carl E. Olson

*All booklets are published*
*thanks to the generosity of the supporters*
*of the Catholic Truth Society*

*ISBN 978 1 78469 662 7*

# Contents

# Introduction

"Christmas", stated Pope Benedict XVI during a General Audience in 2008, "is a privileged opportunity to meditate on the meaning and value of our existence."[1] There is much to contemplate in that single sentence. Do we, for example, think of Christmas as a "privileged opportunity"? As a chance to meditate on the *what* and *why* and *how* of our lives? Our existence? Our place in this world, in this time?

Advent is a time of anticipation, expectation, awakening, reflection. But I knew nothing at all about Advent for the first twenty-five years of my life. Growing up as a young Evangelical Protestant, I certainly looked forward to Christmas, and our family celebrated the birth of Christ. But there really wasn't much preparation; there was no season to help focus my thoughts and heart on what – on Who! – was coming.

Now, having been a Catholic for nearly a quarter of a century, for me Advent has become a favourite time of the liturgical year, for a number of reasons. Benedict XVI captured some of those reasons when he further stated in his audience:

---

[1]  Benedict XVI, General Audience, 17th December 2008.

The approach of this Solemnity helps us on the one hand to reflect on the drama of history in which people, injured by sin, are perennially in search of happiness and of a fulfilling sense of life and death; and on the other, it urges us to meditate on the merciful kindness of God who came to man to communicate to him directly the Truth that saves, and to enable him to partake in his friendship and his life.[2]

Drama. Search. Life. Death. Mercy. Communicate. Truth. Saves. Partake. These are simple, mysterious, powerful words, for they point to the Word, Jesus Christ.

You might say that Advent is the drama that leads to the climax, the search that concludes with the answer, the meditation that is taken up into the Incarnate Word. And the Advent drama does not just look forward, but looks back at salvation history, looks up to the saving heavens, and even looks down at the earthly reality of where we are now. Advent is that time when eternity starts to break into our temporal existence and, if we open our eyes and hearts, breaks into our very being.

Just as creation had marked God's action upon the cosmos, the Incarnation marked the beginning of the world to come. The first Advent was an outpouring of God's grace upon an unsuspecting world. "Grace", wrote French

---

Jesuit Jean Cardinal Daniélou[3] in *The Advent of Salvation: A Comparative Study of Non-Christian Religions and Christianity* (Paulist Press, 1962, quoted more than once in this booklet) is "that bond between mankind and God which can never be broken, because it is founded on the manhood of Christ, in whom Godhead and manhood are henceforth joined together for ever... Christ has brought our humanity into the inmost life of God to stay." We enter that life through baptism, are nourished with the Eucharist and become partakers of the divine nature: "The mystery of history is summed up in God's design of giving his spiritual creatures a share in the life of the Trinity."[4]

That is a startling, humbling, life-changing truth. If we really ponder it, it may well frighten us. Frankly, I think that that might be a good thing, as it would suggest an awakening from the all-too-common dullness of our modern lives. Praise God, we have companions for the journey. There is John the Baptist, who prepared a way for his cousin, the Messiah, by proclaiming that the Kingdom was at hand, and who also prepares the way

---

[3] Jean Daniélou (1905-1974) was a professor at the Institut Catholique in Paris, a prolific scholar and author who occupied a key place in twentieth-century Catholic theology. He is especially known for his dialogue with other world religions, his writings on the Church Fathers and Scripture, and his insights into the nature of divine revelation and Tradition. Daniélou was a theological expert at the Second Vatican Council and in 1969 was made a cardinal by Pope Paul VI.

[4] Jean Daniélou, *The Advent of Salvation*, p. 33.

for us by preparing the way for deeper conversion. He complements Mary, who brings grace by being the Mother of God. Mary's example of faith, of course, should inform our thoughts and shape our actions during Advent. Mary anticipated the birth of her Son for nine months and she now anticipates the birth of the New Creation when he returns in glory.

And then there is the cross. We don't often think of it as a companion during Advent, but it is the way of Christ and of his disciples. We can only long for the coming of Christ and eternal life if we die to ourselves. We must know our place – in both this world and the world to come. God desires a unity of all men, in communion with the Father through the Son. The cross leads to unity; pride leads to death: "The greatest obstacle anyone can put to unity", warns Daniélou, "is to want to make himself the centre of things."

Finally, there is the King and the Kingdom. Jesus came and he will come again, but he is not yet fully made known. "He is not", wrote Daniélou, "fully manifest in mankind as a whole: that is to say, that just as Christ was born according to the flesh in Bethlehem of Judah so must he be born according to the spirit in each of our souls." Advent is anticipation of, preparation for, and contemplation of the King. And that is why Benedict XVI emphasised that we must "prepare ourselves for Christmas with humility and simplicity, making ourselves ready to receive as a gift the light, joy and peace that shine from this mystery".[5]

My hope is that this booklet will help you to prepare, to embrace the drama, to fall more deeply in love with the One who shows us the *what* and *why* and *how* of our lives.

---

[5]  Benedict XVI, General Audience, 17th December 2008.

PART ONE

# MEDITATIONS ON THE
# SUNDAY READINGS

One means of preparation for the coming of the Infant Christ is to delve more deeply into the readings from the Sunday Masses leading up to Christmas. The Sunday readings are proclaimed in a three-year cycle. Each liturgical year begins with the First Sunday of Advent. In 2021, the year this booklet is being published, the First Sunday of Advent begins Cycle C, so Advent 2022 will begin Cycle A, Advent 2023 will begin Cycle B, and so forth. To best make use of this booklet, you may wish to turn to the appropriate cycle of readings so that you are walking through Advent in step with the Church, meditating deeply on the Sunday readings you will hear at Mass this year. (Cycle A: page 12; Cycle B: page 28; Cycle C: page 41.) Christmas each year has the same readings, and preparatory reflections on these appear after Cycle C's Advent readings (on pages 54-57).

# Cycle A: First Sunday of Advent

Readings: *Is* 2:1-5; *Ps* 121:1-2, 3-4, 4-5, 6-7, 8-9;
*Rm* 13:11-14; *Mt* 24:37-44

*Advent is apocalyptic.*

Perhaps you've never thought of it in that way. But today's readings are revealing. I say "revealing" because the word "apocalypse", from the Greek word *apokalupsis*, means "to reveal" or "to unveil". Unfortunately, it has become primarily associated with destruction and violence. But even that understanding is somewhat accurate – even if it only hits part of the target.

Today's Gospel reading, from Matthew 24, is one of three "little apocalypses", the other two being found in Mark 13 and Luke 21. These discourses by Jesus about coming events are complex and difficult, in part because they use methods of Old Testament prophecy in speaking of the future, in part because they refer to both the destruction of the temple (AD 70) and the return of Christ at the end of time. One reason for this is that the destruction of the temple by the Romans was, in a very real sense, the end of the world for devout Jews since the temple embodied God's covenant with the Jewish people and was considered the dwelling place of God's glory. Jesus himself is the new temple (*Rv* 21:22), the fulfilment of everything the Jerusalem temple pointed towards, but most importantly the radical, transforming and eternal communion of God with man.

Speaking to his disciples on the cusp of his Passion, Jesus exhorts them, "Therefore, stay awake!" These are words worth repeating to ourselves throughout the season of Advent. *Wake up! Rouse yourself! Be alert!* Why? Because the King is arriving. The *adventus* – the "arrival" or "coming" of the Lord – is fast approaching. "So, too," Jesus told the disciples, "you also must be prepared, for at an hour you do not expect, the Son of Man will come."

A big problem, as Monsignor Ronald Knox pointed out, is simply this: "We want our Lord to come, but not just yet."[6] Like Augustine, we find ourselves torn between wanting to fully commit ourselves to Christ while also holding on to those things that keep us from him: "Give me chastity and continence, but not yet."[7] Advent is a challenge against comfort, a call to stay awake, an invitation to confession.

"The drama of Advent", wrote Knox in his book *Lightning Meditations*, "is that when we see everything going wrong with the world, we are tempted to be

---

[6] Ronald Knox, *Lightning Meditations* (Sheed & Ward, 1959), p. 7.

[7] St Augustine, *Confessions*, Bk VIII, Ch 7.

indifferent about it all."[8] This drama is also a paradox. Non-Christians (and, alas, many Christians) think that such focus on eternity keeps us from being committed to doing good in this world. But the Apostle Paul would have none of that false notion. He warned the Christians in Rome that they must awake from sleep and "throw off the works of darkness" so that they could "put on the armour of light" and conduct themselves properly. Holiness does not grow when heaven is forgotten; on the contrary, holiness on earth is the fruit of heaven growing within us. Such growth cannot and does not take place without destruction and violence: the dissolution of darkness and the death of sin.

Let's go even further back, to the prophet Isaiah, who wrote of a coming time when all nations would stream towards the house of the Lord. Isaiah recorded a promise of salvation and a warning of judgement. This great work of salvation, however, requires humility and repentance. Walking in the light of the Lord only happens when we accept both his judgement and his mercy, acknowledging our desperate need and his gracious gift.

"Advent is the end of the Old Covenant," explained Fr Hans Urs von Balthasar, "which genuinely looked for God's coming."[9] The advent of the New Covenant took place two thousand years ago. But God's coming also

---

[8] Knox, *Lightning Meditations*, p. 8.

[9] Hans Urs Von Balthasar, *You Crown the Year with Your Goodness* (Ignatius Press, 1989).

takes place at every moment, which is why St Paul wrote of the nearness of salvation while warning against the darkness of sinful pursuits. And it will be completed at the final advent, the second coming, which is why Jesus exhorted the disciples to be prepared at every hour for the hour – the hour of revealing, of apocalypse.

# Second Sunday of Advent

Readings: *Is* 11:1-10; *Ps* 72:1-2, 7-8, 12-13, 17;
*Rm* 15:4-9; *Mt* 3:1-12

*Repent, repent, repent.*

If you saw John the Baptist preaching on a street corner, what might you think of him? He would be a wiry man, wild in appearance, bearded and dressed in rough clothing. His message would be direct, but also mysterious: "Repent, for the Kingdom of heaven is at hand!" He would offer free baptisms and would, from time to time, have less than kind words for various authorities who watched him baptise.

He would be, in today's terms, a troublemaker, a religious fanatic, a fundamentalist, a narrow-minded zealot.

Jesus, however, told his disciples "Truly, I say to you, among those born of women there has arisen no one greater than John the Baptist". (*Mt* 11:11). This wasn't merely the affection of the Saviour for his cousin, but a striking assertion of John's place in salvation history. John the Baptist, like so many of the Old Testament prophets, was contrary and confrontational. He drew attention to things usually passed over in polite society, especially the reality of sin and the need for repentance. He denounced hypocrisy, spiritual sloth and injustice. And today's Gospel reading – which contains the first mention of John in Scripture – describes him as the final and greatest forerunner of the Messiah: "A voice of one crying out in the desert…."

In his book *The Advent of Salvation: A Comparative Study of Non-Christian Religions and Christianity*, Jean Cardinal Daniélou wrote:

> Since the coming of Christ goes on for ever – he is always he who is to come in the world and in the Church – there is always an advent going on, and this advent is filled by John the Baptist. It is John the Baptist's peculiar grace that he prepares the way for what is about to happen.[10]

The Church has long made the connection between John the Baptist and Advent because John perfectly symbolises – or, better, lives and expresses – the key themes of this season: anticipation, preparation, humility, repentance. His baptism was one of repentance, but he readily acknowledged that it would give way to the baptism of "the Holy Spirit and fire" offered by Jesus.

John, who was filled with the Holy Spirit even before he was born, knew that his work was to prepare himself

---

[10] Jean Daniélou, *The Advent of Salvation*, p. 79.

and others for the One who would offer the fullness of the Holy Spirit. "The fire of the Spirit dwells in him", states the *Catechism of the Catholic Church*, "and makes him the forerunner of the coming Lord" (*CCC* 718). He, like all of the prophets, pointed to the Messiah. And he, like all of God's faithful, did the bidding of the Saviour. But John, the *Catechism* also points out, was more than a prophet, for "with John the Baptist, the Holy Spirit begins the restoration to man of 'the divine likeness'" (*CCC* 720).

Drawing again from modern parlance, we might say that John the Baptist worked himself out of a job. Jesus, having declared the greatness of John, remarks, "Yet the one who is least in the kingdom of heaven is greater than he" (*Mt* 11:11). How so? The greatness of John was in his faithfulness to the call of proclaiming the Son of God. But that does not match the greatness of those who, by grace, have been baptised into the life of the Son of God. They are filled with the divine life of God, made possible by the redemptive work of the cross. The New Covenant is greater than the Old Covenant, and it establishes the Kingdom of God, which is what John the Baptist and the other prophets anticipated and desired.

The heart of John is revealed beautifully in his statement, found in John's Gospel, "He must increase, but I must decrease" (*Jn* 3:30). That is, I think, a perfect prayer for Advent. It speaks of a heart completely given to the Holy Spirit. It describes the essence of being a disciple of

Jesus Christ. It reveals a man who speaks the truth in the wilderness, regardless of what everyone else on the street corner might think of him.

# Cycle A: Third Sunday of Advent

Readings: *Is* 35:1-6a, 10; *Ps* 146:6-7, 8-9, 9-10;
*Jm* 5:7-10; *Mt* 11:2-11

*First, awaken. Then repent. Now rejoice.*

Those have been the central themes during these three Sundays of Advent. On the first Sunday, we heard Jesus exhort the disciples, "Therefore, stay awake!" Last Sunday we heard John the Baptist, the voice in the wilderness, preaching "Repent!"

Today, on Gaudete Sunday (from the Latin word for "rejoice"), we hear of joy, exultation, glory and gladness. "Be strong," declared the prophet Isaiah, "fear not!" Looking to the future, anticipating a time of peace and abundance, he gave several reasons for his call to joy. First, there is the "glory of the Lord, the splendour of our God". Recognising God's existence and acknowledging his overwhelming beauty and power is foundational to any real joy; without this knowledge, joy is fleeting. Then there is God's gift of salvation: "Here is your God, he comes with vindication; with divine recompense he comes to save you." God is not just magnificent, he is magnanimous; he is not only great, he is giving. Finally, this gift of salvation is cause for everlasting joy for it means that we are meant to enter Zion, to come into his presence with thanksgiving – for all of eternity.

But no joy can be found if we are not awake; those who slumber cannot sing. And there is no joy for the sinner, for those who refuse to repent cannot be reborn or renewed. "The power of rejoicing is always a fair test of a man's moral condition", observed Archbishop Fulton Sheen. "No man can be happy on the outside who is already unhappy on the inside… As sorrow is attendant on sin, so joy is the companion of holiness."[11]

Today's reading from James anticipates one of the serious challenges for everyone who has awoken and repented and now waits: impatience. "Be patient, therefore, brothers," writes James, who was addressing Christians dispersed outside of Palestine, "until the coming of the Lord" (*Jm* 5:7). He is emphatic on this point: "You also, be patient." Impatience has a way of eating at our resolve, our hope, our sense of perspective. When impatience takes over, we are tempted to think we will be better off doing things our way, in our time and according to our wisdom. We begin to complain, and our resolve wilts. Impatience let loose will eventually attack our faith and destroy our peace.

---

[11] Fulton John Sheen, *The Electronic Christian: 105 Readings from Fulton J. Sheen* (Macmillan, 1979), p. 97.

St Teresa of Avila warned of this, writing:

> Hope, O my soul, hope. You know neither the day nor
> the hour. Watch carefully, for everything passes quickly,
> even though your impatience makes doubtful what is
> certain, and turns a very short time into a long one.
> Dream that the more you struggle, the more you prove
> the love that you bear your God, and the more you will
> rejoice one day with your Beloved, in a happiness and
> rapture that can never end. (Cited in *CCC* 1821)

But what of John the Baptist? Did he give in to impatience?
Today's Gospel seems, at first blush, to suggest so. After
all, the imprisoned prophet sent his disciples to Jesus,
asking, "Are you the one who is to come?" But John,
who never wavered in delivering his message or standing
his ground, did this for the benefit of others. "John asks
this not because he is ignorant," explained St Jerome,
"but to guide others who are ignorant and say to them,
'Behold, the Lamb of God, who takes away the sins of the
world!'"[12] They were attached to John, but they needed to
be transformed by Christ. In sending them to Jesus, John
was shaking them awake.

John the Baptist was a prophet – "and more than a
prophet" – but he was not the Saviour. He announced
that the Kingdom of heaven was at hand, but he was not

---

[12] Thomas C. Oden and Cindy Crosby, *Ancient Christian Devotional:
Lectionary Cycle A, Volume 1* (InterVarsity Press, 2007), p. 24.

the King. John's greatness came from his faithful, joyful proclamation of the greatness of the Lord. Like him, we are called to rejoice in the glory, the gift and the goodness of God.

# Cycle A: Fourth Sunday of Advent

Readings: *Is* 7:10-14; *Ps* 24:1-2, 3-4, 5-6;
*Rm* 1:1-7; *Mt* 1:18-24

*"Looking on thee, O Unwedded One, and dreading
a hidden wedlock, O Sinless One, the chaste Joseph
was riven in mind with a storm of doubts".*[13]

That is how the anxious state of Joseph, as he considered
what to do with his young and pregnant betrothed, was
poetically described by the unknown author of the great
Akathist hymn c. sixth century to the Blessed Virgin Mary.
Joseph, following the usual Jewish practice, had been
covenanted to Mary; their engagement was, for all intents
and purposes, as legally binding as marriage. According to
Jewish law, this meant the engagement could only end in
one of two ways: divorce or death (*Dt* 24:1-4).

Although devotion to St Joseph has grown tremendously
in recent centuries, it is still easy to overlook both the
tremendous decisions he faced and the great character

---

[13] Luigi Gambero, *Mary and the Fathers of the Church: The Blessed
Virgin Mary in Patristic Thought* (Ignatius Press, 1999), p. 344.

he demonstrated in making those decisions. Today's reading from the Gospel of Matthew describes Joseph as a "righteous man". This is not some vague reference to Joseph simply being a nice guy, but is a direct recognition of his whole-hearted commitment to the Law. "And it will be righteousness for us", said the Hebrews at Mount Sinai, upon being given the Decalogue, or Ten Commandments, "if we are careful to do all this commandment before the Lord our God, as he has commanded us" (*Dt* 6:25). Joseph was careful to follow the commandments; he desired to love and serve God completely.

Yet he was faced with a gut-wrenching, scandalous situation: a young bride who was already pregnant. However, Joseph was "unwilling to expose Mary to shame" and had decided to divorce her – or, better translated, "to send her away quietly". Some of the Church Fathers and Doctors believed that Joseph had suspected Mary of adultery.[14] Others thought that he had withheld moral judgement, being genuinely perplexed by the strange situation. And some, including St Thomas Aquinas, believed that Joseph knew of the miraculous nature of Mary's pregnancy from the start, and had sought to separate himself from her because of a deep sense of unworthiness.[15]

---

[14] John Saward, *Cradle of Redeeming Love: The Theology of the Christmas Mystery* (Ignatius Press, 2002), p. 12.

[15] St Thomas Aquinas, *Summa Theologica*, Part III ("Tertia Pars").

So we don't know what Joseph knew prior to the angel of the Lord appearing to him. Rather remarkably, we also don't know what Joseph may have said, simply because not one word that he uttered is recorded! But we do learn some important things from the words of the angel, as well as from Joseph's actions.

The angel provided Joseph with three essential gifts and truths. First, the divine messenger granted him the gift of peace: "Do not be afraid to take Mary your wife into your home." The coming of the Lord is always a gift of peace to those who love and serve him. Secondly, he told Joseph that there was a divine plan in place: Mary will give birth to Jesus – which means "Yahweh saves" – who will save his people from sin. Joseph would surely have recognised this as a description of the long-awaited Messiah. Finally, the angel provided the prophetic background to this stunning event, the passage from Isaiah 7, today's reading from the Old Testament. This would have further reinforced the reality of the divine plan.

Joseph, in turn, did three things. He thought, first and foremost, about Mary and her well-being. He acted justly, without concern for himself, even though he had every legal right to be upset. A good husband puts the needs and reputation of his wife before his own. Second, he placed his trust and hope in God's promise. Although we never hear any words from Joseph, we are told of his actions. A godly man walks the talk, but with a minimum of talk!

Third, Joseph embraced the daunting task of being the foster father of the Son of God. Why? Because he trusted in God despite the strangeness of the situation.

And what is the conclusion of the verse of the Akathist hymn quoted above? "But learning that your conception was of the Holy Spirit, he cried out: 'Alleluia!'" Alleluia, indeed!

# Cycle B: First Sunday of Advent

Readings: *Is* 63:16b-17, 19b, 64:2-7; *Ps* 80:2-3, 15-16, 18-19; *1 Co* 1:3-9; *Mk* 13:33-37

*Awaken and await!*

What is Advent? Pope Benedict XVI, in a homily given on the First Sunday of Advent in 2008, noted that the Latin word *adventus* is one that "could be translated by 'arrival', 'coming' or 'presence'" (Pastoral Visit to the Basilica of Saint Lawrence Outside the Walls, homily of his holiness Benedict XVI, First Sunday of Advent, 30th November 2008). It reminds us of the first coming of Christ two thousand years ago, as well as the present coming of Christ in and through the Church, especially in the Eucharist. It also orientates us to the future coming of Christ, at the moment of our death and at the end of time.

Pope Benedict XVI further stated that Advent is "a time of expectation and hope, a privileged time for listening and reflection, as long as we let ourselves be guided by the liturgy, which invites us to advance to meet the Lord who comes."

Today's readings present many of these interrelated words and truths so that we might contemplate more deeply the meaning – for today and for eternity – of this great season. There are seven words in particular that I will focus on here: the first three are words addressed by man to God; the next three are words addressed by God to man; and the final word has to do with God meeting man face-to-face.

The first three are from the prophet Isaiah and Psalm 80: return, come, and save. The reading from the Book of Isaiah is taken from a lengthy poem of confession and lament (*Is* 63:7–64:11) written after the return from exile in 538 BC, prior to the rebuilding of the temple in Jerusalem. There are two intertwined confessions in the passage, one being an honest admission of grave sin and the other a declaration of trust in God's saving power and fatherly mercy. "Return," the author beseeches, "for the sake of your servants," as he longs for a palpable, even shocking, display of God's presence among his people. God, however, had hidden his face from the sinful people; yet, despite the silence, there is hope that God, being a father, will again take up and mould his people as a potter moulds clay.

Similar expressions of penance and hope are voiced in the responsorial psalm, also a lament. "Lord, make us turn to you," cries the Psalmist, "let us see your face and we shall be saved." To see the face of God is to be cleansed of sin and embraced as a child of the Father. The psalm is filled with a yearning that finds fulfilment in the Incarnation: "Rouse your power and come to save us." It points to that moment in time when the power of the Most

High overshadowed Mary, who became pregnant with a son who "will save his people from their sins" (*Lk* 1:35; *Mt* 1:21). In all of this, God initiates; man calls out for mercy, but must wait until God acts.

The next three words or exhortations are variations on the same central theme: wait, watch, be alert. The Apostle Paul assumed that waiting "for the revelation of our Lord Jesus Christ" is the constant and expected status of every disciple of Christ. Jesus repeatedly told his disciples, "Be on your guard" (*Mk* 13:9, 23, 33, 37). This is what Advent is all about: being watchful, attentive, and alert. This means being aware of our need for repentance and our need for a deeper fellowship with Jesus Christ our Lord.

We are to be patient "until the coming of the Lord" (*Jm* 5:7), and to "waiting for the mercy of our Lord Jesus Christ that leads to eternal life" (*Jude* 1:21). In doing so, we express our belief in the first Advent, when God became man, and in the coming Advent, when the God-man will come again in glory. Which brings us to the seventh word: "day". That is, the "day of our Lord Jesus Christ", when the Son of God will judge the living and the dead, rendering to each man according to his works and response to God's grace. "The Advent cry of hope", says Benedict XVI, "then expresses...our extreme need of salvation."[16]

---

[16] Celebration of First Vespers of the First Sunday of Advent, homily of his holiness Benedict XVI, St Peter's Basilica, 29th November 2008.

# Cycle B: Second Sunday of Advent

Readings: *Is* 40:1-5, 9-11; *Ps* 85:9-12, 13-14;
*2 P* 3:8-14; *Mk* 1:1-8

*"In my beginning is my end."*[17]

The line in the heading above opens "East Coker", the
second section of T.S. Eliot's poetic masterpiece, *Four
Quartets*. It is followed by a haunting, elegiac reflection
on the fragile and transitory nature of life as seen in the
cycle of life and death in nature.

What is the meaning of our short lives? What hope is
man given in this passing world? In whom shall we trust
for our salvation? These questions are always with us,
but gain in poignancy during Advent. While the entire
liturgical year is ultimately orientated towards all that is
heavenly and everlasting, Advent is especially focused on
the end of our earthly lives.

And, just as Eliot indicates, the beginning points to
The End, a fact presented by St Mark in his direct, urgent
style: "The beginning of the gospel of Jesus Christ the
Son of God." More than a heading or title, this is a bold

---

[17] T.S. Eliot, "East Coker" from *Four Quartets* (Harcourt, 1943).

proclamation of the good news and joyful tidings of the life, death and resurrection of Jesus Christ. It is the inspired declaration that the man Jesus of Nazareth is indeed the Messiah, the anointed one. He has come to deliver his people from sin and death, and to establish the reign of God among men.

This announcement is made within the Gospel of Mark by St Peter, a Jew following in the footsteps of Jesus (*Mk* 8:29), and by the centurion, a Gentile standing at the foot of the Cross. In this way, the universal nature of the New Covenant is revealed and professed.

But the first announcement in Mark's Gospel is from the lips of John the Baptist, the voice crying out in the desert. John is the last of the Old Testament prophets, but he is "more than a prophet" (*Lk* 7:26), a mysterious figure whose strange physical appearance is coupled with a striking message: "I have baptised you with water; he will baptise you with the Holy Spirit."

Ritual cleansing with water was not new to the Jews, but this baptism in the Jordan River was clearly meant to be different. The Jordan River, of course, was significant in its symbolism. The forty years of exodus in the wilderness had ended many hundreds of years earlier when Joshua led the Israelites across the river and into the promised land (*Jos* 3). The Messiah, John indicates, is going to call the people to enter through water into a new promised land, a new Zion, a new Jerusalem.

This beginning, rooted in the Old Covenant, provides the grace and forgiveness necessary for the end, what is described by St Peter as the "new heavens and a new earth in which righteousness dwells" (*2 P* 3:13). But this end is already present in the beginning. In the words of Eliot in "East Coker", "Home is where one starts from." Baptism brings us home; it destroys sin, restores the divine life of God, and makes man a son of God. For "just as the gestation of our first birth took place in water," according to the *Catechism of the Catholic Church*, "so the water of Baptism truly signifies that our birth into the divine life is given to us in the Holy Spirit" (*CCC* 694).

This is the comfort spoken of by Isaiah in today's first reading: it is the peace, truth, justice and salvation desired by the Psalmist.

In listening to the cry of John the Baptist we hear the message of Advent. Prepare the way of the Lord by repenting of sin and embracing the divine life granted in baptism. Go to Confession, spend additional time in prayer, and proclaim the gospel in word and deed. By spending more time in prayer and contemplation, we open the way for the guidance of the Holy Spirit. "We must be still and still moving", wrote Eliot of this spiritual purification, "Into another intensity/For a further union, a deeper communion".

And then we will recognise more deeply *this* truth, which concludes "East Coker": "In my end is my beginning."

# Cycle B: Third Sunday of Advent

Readings: *Is* 61:1-2a, 10-11; *Lk* 1:46-48, 49-50, 53-54;
*1 Th* 5:16-24; *Jn* 1:6-8, 19-28

*"My spirit exults in God, my Saviour."* (*Lk* 1:47)

Gaudete Sunday is a day of joy and rejoicing (the Latin word for "rejoice" is *gaudere*), offering an even more heightened sense of promise and anticipation as Christmas approaches. This Third Sunday of Advent, observed Monsignor Ronald Knox,

> interrupts us when we are all telling one another that the world is dust and ashes, the ante-room of eternity. Joy is woven into the pattern as well as sorrow; to rejoice is more than a grudging permission; it is, at times, a sort of Christian duty.

There is a temptation to associate joy solely with our emotions. But joy, while certainly shown at times through our emotional responses, goes deeper. It is the response of our heart, mind and soul to the grace of God, the recognition of his saving power, mercy and love. In the opening chapter of the Gospel of Luke, the Blessed Virgin

Mary says, "My soul rejoices in my God", or "My spirit exults in God, my Saviour."

This echoes the joyful song of Hannah, who said, "My heart exults in the Lord, my horn is exalted in the Lord", after having dedicated her son Samuel to the Lord (*1 S* 1:27–2:1). The "spirit" is the essence of life, and Luke is likely emphasising the rational, contemplative mind.

In short, to rejoice is to recognise and embrace the truth about God's work. Thus, the Apostle Paul told the Christians at Thessalonica, "Rejoice always. Pray without ceasing." But how can we always be joyful and never stop praying? By recognising that being a Christian does not require us to feel a certain way at all times, but rather to think with the mind of Christ and obey the will of God. A husband and wife truly dedicated to their marriage do not attempt merely to maintain the emotions experienced on their honeymoon, but pursue an even deeper nuptial bond, rooted in a committed, willed love.

Throughout Advent, two people are held up as examples of this faithful love. The first, of course, is John the Baptist, the focus of both last week's and today's Gospel readings. The emphasis in today's reading from the opening chapter of the Gospel of John is on testimony, or witness. The Greek word – *martyria* – for "testify" or "witness" is also the root word for "martyr", and it appears nearly thirty times in the Fourth Gospel, as well as several times in the Book of Revelation.

What does John the Baptist testify to? The person of Jesus Christ, described in the prologue of the Fourth Gospel as light: "to the light, so that all might believe through him". The Apostle John had also witnessed the light of Christ; in fact, he described himself as the "disciple whom Jesus loved" (*Jn* 13:23; 20:2; 21:7, 20). But John the Baptist, the cousin of Jesus, had a most unique testimony, for he had recognised the Saviour while both were still in the womb (*Lk* 1:41). He then gave witness not only by word but also by deed: first, through preaching and baptism, then finally through martyrdom (*Mk* 6:17-29).

The second person, now emerging more fully in the Advent readings, is the Mother of God. Her "Magnificat" is also a joyful expression of witness, the testimony of the perfect disciple: "My soul proclaims the greatness of the Lord; my spirit rejoices in God my saviour." Mary, wrote St Bede, proclaimed both her humility and God's holiness:

> She demonstrates that in her own judgement she was indeed Christ's humble handmaid, but with respect to heavenly grace she pronounces herself all at once lifted up and glorified to such a degree that rightly her pre-eminent blessedness would be marvelled at by the voices of all nations.[18]

---

[18] St Bede, *Homilies on the Gospels*, 1.4.

This, then, is the source and focus of joy: God has come and is coming to save us from sin, despair and death. As St Paul explained, God brings the gift of holiness, so that we may, "whole spirit and soul and body, be kept blameless at the coming of our Lord Jesus Christ" (*1 Th* 5:23).

# Cycle B: Fourth Sundy of Advent

Readings: *2 S* 7:1-5, 8b-12, 14a, 16; *Ps* 89:2-3, 4-5, 27, 29;
*Rm* 16:25-27; *Lk* 1:26-38

*"Would you build me a house to dwell in?"* (*2 S* 7:5)

This question, asked of King David by God, seems simple enough, yet is bursting with implications and suggestions that only come to completion many centuries later with the conception and birth of Jesus Christ, the Son of David. Having settled into his palace, King David recognised how inappropriate it was to live in comfort while the ark of the covenant remained in a tent.

The significance of David's sensitivity to the situation should not be overlooked. This was the same man who expressed deep reverence for the ark (*2 S* 6:9), who danced in exultation as it was brought into the city of Jerusalem, and who then offered sacrifices as "he blessed the people in the name of the Lord of hosts" (*2 S* 6:12-19).

The Dominican theologian Fr Yves Congar wrote that David had a "sensitive and profound religious spirit" and that, for him, "the religious motive was paramount, all-inclusive, and absolutely pure."[19] So it is understandable that David wished to build a temple, and it is no surprise that the prophet Nathan thought well of the idea.

But God responded with a word of recollection and of promise. First, he reminded David of the past: it was God who chose David, who cared for him, who protected and guided him, and who conquered his enemies. "I have been with you", he said, "wherever you went." The ark and the tent did not contain God, but were visible signs of God's presence with his people. God "makes his own temple by dwelling in the midst of his people", wrote Congar, "and his presence cannot fail to be supremely active."

Then God pointed to the future, when he would build and establish the house of David from which would come an heir and a kingdom. This was fulfilled, in temporal terms, through Solomon, who did build the great temple in Jerusalem. But, of course, Solomon sank into sin and eventually the people were taken into exile. The perfect fulfilment would not come through military might and physical conquest, but through humility and holiness, through a virgin "betrothed to a man named Joseph, of the house of David."

God was still with his people; he was especially with Mary in a most unique way: "Hail, full of grace! The Lord is with you." John Paul II, in the 1987 encyclical devoted

---

[19] Yves Congar, *The Mystery of the Temple* (Newman Press, 1962).

to the Blessed Mother, *Redemptoris Mater*, noted that: "The fullness of grace announced by the angel means the gift of God himself." God was with his people at Mount Sinai and throughout their forty years in the desert. Now, the angel told the maiden, the Holy Spirit will come and the "power of the Most High will overshadow you", just as, in the words of John Paul II, "at the time of Moses and the Patriarchs the cloud covered the presence of God". This overshadowing is the same mysterious manifestation of God's presence that is described in Exodus 40:35: "Moses could not enter the tent of meeting, because the cloud settled down upon it and the glory of the Lord filled the tabernacle."

Mary, then, is the new tabernacle. Through her perfect humility and faith, she became the Mother of God and the Mother "in the order of grace". God, who cannot be contained by anything or anyone, came into the world through the tabernacle of Mary. "For the first time in the plan of salvation and because his Spirit had prepared her, the Father found the *dwelling place* where his Son and his Spirit could dwell among men" (*CCC* 721). David longed to build a temple but only God could build a house to dwell in, for our sake and for his glory.

In the words of an Eastern hymn: "Mary, Mother of God, honourable tabernacle of sweet ointments, make me through your prayers a chosen vessel that I may receive the sanctification of your son."

# Cycle C: First Sunday of Advent

Readings: *Jr* 33:14-16; *Ps* 25:4-5, 8-9, 10, 14;
*1 Th* 3:12-4:2; *Lk* 21:25-28, 34-36

*"We preach not one advent only of Christ, but a second also, far more glorious than the former. For the former gave a view of his patience; but the latter brings with it the crown of a divine Kingdom."*[20]

The term "advent", as we will see, is drawn from the New Testament, but when St Cyril (named a Doctor of the Church in 1883 by Pope Leo XIII) was writing his famous catechetical lectures, the season of Advent was just starting to emerge in fledgling form in Spain and Gaul. During the fifth century, Christians in parts of Western Europe began observing a period of ascetical practices leading up to the feasts of Christmas and Epiphany. Advent was observed in Rome beginning in the sixth century, and it was sometimes called the "pre-Christmas Lent", a time of fasting, more frequent prayer, and additional liturgies.

---

[20] St Cyril of Jerusalem in *Nicene and Post-Nicene Fathers: Second Series, Volume VII Cyril of Jerusalem, Gregory Nazianzen*, ed. Philip Schaff (Cosimo Classics, 2007), p. 104.

One of the prayers of the Roman Missal from those early centuries is, "Stir up our hearts, O Lord, to prepare the ways of thy only-begotten Son: that by his coming we may be able to serve him with purified minds." This echoes today's reading from St Paul's first letter to the Christians in Thessalonica, in which he exhorts them "to strengthen your hearts, to be blameless before our God and Father at the coming of our Lord Jesus with all his holy ones. Amen."

The Greek word used by St Paul for "coming" is *parousia*, which means "presence" or "coming to a place". The Vulgate translation of the phrase "the coming of our Lord Jesus" (*1 Th* 3:13) is rendered "in *adventu* Domini". The word *parousia* appears twenty-four times in the New Testament, almost always in reference to the coming or presence of the Lord. It appears in Matthew 24 four times, the only place the term appears in the Gospels; that chapter records the Olivet Discourse, Jesus's prophetic warnings about a coming time of trial, destruction and "the coming of the Son of Man" (*Mt* 24:27). Today's Gospel reading, from Luke 21, is a parallel passage, warning of distress, startling heavenly signs and "the Son of Man coming in a cloud with power and great glory".

What connection is there between the foment of earthly tribulation and cosmic upheaval, and preparations to celebrate Christ's birth? If we consider the Christmas story cleared of sentimental wrappings, we see events as dramatic, raw, bloody and joyous as can be imagined: the birth of Christ, the slaughter of the innocents, the praise of angels, the murderous rage of Herod. Christmas is about birth, but also death; about rejoicing, but also rejection. It is the story of God desired and God denied. It is the story every man has to encounter because it is the story of God's radical plan of salvation, the entrance of divinity into the dusty ruts and twisting corridors of human history.

Advent orientates us to the heart of the Nativity – not in a merely metaphorical way, but through the reality of the liturgy, the Eucharist, the sacramental life of the Church. It is a wake-up call, perhaps even an alarm rousing us from "carousing and drunkenness and the anxieties of daily life". The birth of Christ caught many by surprise. Likewise, we can find ourselves trapped in the darkness of dull living and missing Christ's call to raise our heads as salvation approaches.

"Advent calls believers to become aware of this truth and to act accordingly", said Pope Benedict XVI in a homily marking the beginning of Advent in 2006. "It rings out as a salutary appeal in the days, weeks and months that repeat: Awaken! Remember that God comes! Not yesterday, not tomorrow, but today, now!" Jesus told his disciples to be vigilant, prepared and prayerful.

The same is true for his disciples today, so they might escape the tribulations of spiritual darkness and stand prepared before the Son of Man, the son of Mary.

# Cycle C: Second Sunday of Advent

Readings: *Ba* 5:1-9; *Ps* 126:1-2, 2-3, 4-5, 6;
*Ph* 1:4-6, 8-11; *Lk* 3:1-6

*"There are three distinct comings of the Lord of which
I know, his coming to people, his coming into people,
and his coming against people."*[21]

St Bernard of Clairvaux, the great twelfth-century Doctor
of the Church, added that Christ's "coming to people and
his coming against people are too well known to need
elucidation." Since, however, today's Gospel reading
mentions both groups – those Christ comes to and those he
comes against – a bit of elucidation is in order.

St Luke took pains to situate the fact of the Incarnation
within human history. He did so by providing the names of
several different rulers, beginning with Caesar Augustus
(*Lk* 2:1), who reigned from 27 BC to AD 14, and who was
ruler of the Roman Empire when Jesus was born.

In today's Gospel, the evangelist situates John the
Baptist's bold announcement of Christ's coming in the
fifteenth year of Tiberius Caesar. Tiberius, the stepson of

---

[21] St Bernard of Clairvaux from an Advent sermon.

Augustus, reigned from AD 14 to AD 37. Pontius Pilate was appointed procurator of Judaea by Tiberius in AD 26, and served in that post for ten years. Those men and the others mentioned by St Luke – Herod, Philip, Lysanias, and the high priests Annas and Caiaphas – ruled the known world while the ruler of all creation walked the dusty roads of Palestine and announced that the Kingdom of God was at hand. The Roman rulers were ruthless and often violent men who established rule and kept order through military might and political power. They did, in fact, establish and keep a sort of peace – the *Pax Romana* – which lasted about two centuries (27 BC to *c*. AD 180).

Yet that peace was both uneasy and fragile; it had been won by the sword and often relied on fear, intimidation, and persecution. St Luke's mention of these rulers was, on one hand, meant to support the historical nature of his "orderly account", which was to be "a narrative of the things that have been accomplished among us" (see *Lk* 1: 1-4). But, on the other hand, it was also meant to establish a deliberate comparison and contrast between the rulers of this world and the ruler of nations, between the kings of earthly realms and the King of kings.

The Roman rulers used force and relied upon fear, but the Incarnate Word came with humility and love. Emperors were announced and escorted by armed soldiers, but the birth of the Christ child was announced by heavenly hosts offering songs of praise, not swords or spears. "What the angel proposes to the shepherds is another *kyrios* [Lord]," notes Bishop Robert Barron in *The Priority of Christ*, "the Messiah Jesus, whose rule will constitute a true justice because it is conditioned not by fear but by love and forgiveness".[22] The Lord came against injustice, fear, violence and death, and would himself experience each of those dreadful realities for the sake of all men. Such would be "the salvation of God" spoken of by John the Baptist, who quoted from Isaiah's beautiful and moving hymn-like reflection on the glory and goodness of God (*Is* 40).

John, like Isaiah, was pointing towards the comfort, peace and joy that only God can give. Yet the final rest and joy is not yet fully known. We live, St Bernard explained, during the time of the "third coming" of Christ, between the Incarnation and the final coming, or advent, when all men will finally see the pierced but glorious Lord. "The intermediate coming is a hidden one; in it only the elect see the Lord within their own selves, and they are saved."

Christ comes to us in spirit and in power; he most especially comes to us under the appearance of bread and wine. "Because this coming lies between the other two," wrote St Bernard, "it is like a road on which we travel from the first coming to the last."

That winding road is the way of the Lord, the path of Advent.

---

[22] Robert Barron, *The Priority of Christ: Toward a Postliberal Catholicism* (Brazos Press, 2007), p. 94.

# Cycle C: Third Sunday of Advent

Readings: *Zp* 3:14-18a; *Is* 12:2-3, 4, 5-6;
*Ph* 4:4-7; *Lk* 3:10-18

*"Great joy has in it the sense of immortality".*[23]

Joy, like love, hope and goodness, cannot be adequately or convincingly explained through material processes or properties. Joy is a gift pointing to a transcendent giver. And that giver is the Lord, the giver of both natural and supernatural life. Gaudete Sunday is a day of joy and rejoicing (the Latin word for "rejoice" is *gaudere*), and the readings reflect this theme. The reading from the prophet Zephaniah contains an exultant call for Israel to shout and sing for joy. Why? Because the Lord had staved off judgement, rebuffed Israel's enemies, and stood as King and Saviour in the midst of the chosen people.

The responsorial psalm, from Isaiah, echoes the same: "Cry out with joy and gladness, for among you is the great and Holy One of Israel." And the Epistle, from St Paul's letter to the Philippians, has a hymnic, even rhapsodic,

---

[23] G.K. Chesterton, *The Collected Works of G.K. Chesterton*, Volume 1 (Ignatius Press, 1990), p. 94.

quality: "Rejoice in the Lord always. I shall say it again: rejoice!" The reason, again, is due to the immediacy of God's intimate, life-giving presence: "The Lord is near."

The Gospel reading does not directly refer to joy, but instead anticipates and points, through the words of John the Baptist, towards the source of joy. The anticipation has two different but connected qualities. The first is external and focuses on the natural moral virtues; it is drawn out through the question asked by the crowds, the tax collectors and the soldiers: "What should we do?" John's response, in essence, is that they should act justly towards their neighbours and those in their communities.

Treating others with respect and acting with justice are virtuous actions. However, they are lacking to the degree that they are solely human. The need for something more is hinted at in the raised expectations of the people, who "were asking in their hearts whether John might be the Christ". Having recognised the need for natural goodness, they now hunger for supernatural goodness – that is, for the Christ. Having tasted the joy that comes from seeking the good for others, they wish to receive the joy that comes from the good given by God (cf. *CCC* 1804).

The distinction and relationship between the human and supernatural virtues is highlighted further in comparing the baptism of John to the baptism of the Messiah. The first is an external sign, a washing of water, symbolising the need for purity and the desire for holiness. The second is an efficacious sign, a sacrament, which accomplishes what it signifies. "By the action of Christ and the power of the Holy Spirit", explains the *Catechism*, the sacraments "make present efficaciously the grace that they signify" (*CCC* 1084).

What about the fire mentioned by John? While water symbolises birth and life, "fire symbolises the transforming energy of the Holy Spirit's actions" (*CCC* 696). Both water and fire can destroy, but both are also necessary for life. And in the case of baptism, this life is supernatural, divine, Trinitarian. In baptism, original sin is destroyed, the chasm between God and man is closed, and the soul is ignited with divine fire. Joined in the death of the Son (cf. *Rm* 6), those who are baptised are transformed by the Holy Spirit into sons of God, made anew for the glory of the Father, and prepared for life in the new heavens and new earth.

Here, then, is the source and heart of our Advent joy. The season anticipates the celebration of Christ's birth, but it also illuminates the purpose of the Incarnation: to remove judgement, to destroy sin and death, and to grant intimate, life-giving communion with God. "All seek joy," said St John Chrysostom, "but it is not found on earth."[24] It is found instead in the Son, who comes from heaven to earth – to the crowds, tax collectors, soldiers, and us. Great joy flows from immortality. *Rejoice!*

---

[24] *The Book of Ancient Wisdom: Over 500 Inspiring Quotations from the Greeks and Romans*, ed. Bill Bradfield (Courier Corporation, 2012), p. 43.

# Cycle C: Fourth Sunday of Advent

Readings: *Mi* 5:1-4a; *Ps* 80:2-3, 15-16, 18-19;
*Heb* 10:5-10; *Lk* 1:39-45

*"By singing praise to your maternity, we all exalt you
as a spiritual temple, Mother of God! For the One who
dwelt within your womb, the Lord who holds all things
in his hands, sanctified you, glorified you, and taught
all men to sing to you".*[25]

St Augustine, in his treatise "On Holy Virginity", made
this profound, even startling, statement: "Thus also her
nearness as a mother would have been of no profit to Mary,
had she not borne Christ in her heart after a more blessed
manner than in her flesh."

In that single line, the great Doctor anticipated
the objections voiced by many Protestants while also
explaining the honour and love shown by Catholics (and
Eastern Orthodox) for the *Theotokos*, the Mother of God. I
heard and repeated, while growing up in a Protestant home
of Fundamentalist persuasion, many of those objections:
"Mary was just an ordinary woman", "Mary was not

---

[25] Extract from the Akathist hymn to the Blessed Virgin Mary.

sinless", and, of course, "Catholics worship Mary!" People would sometimes go to extremes to avoid any appearance of praise for Mary. A close relative once told me that Mary had merely been a "biological vessel" for the baby Jesus!

Two things changed my mind: reading actual Catholic teaching about Mary and re-reading Scripture. The first came from a sense of fairness towards what I didn't know; the second came from a growing humility about what I thought I knew. Sure, I had read the opening chapters of the Gospel of Luke many times. But I must have read it dozens of times more before I began to slowly comprehend the astonishment of the Annunciation, the wonder of Elizabeth's ecstatic greeting, the magnitude of the "Magnificat".

Today's Gospel reading follows the Annunciation and immediately precedes the "Canticle of Mary". The young Mary, told by Gabriel that she had found favour with God and would bear a son, eventually sets out to see Elizabeth, also pregnant with a son. Having already been confirmed by a heavenly messenger of God, Mary was then confirmed by her own flesh and blood in words heard and repeated by countless faithful through the centuries: "Blessed are you among women and blessed is the fruit of your womb." To be blessed is to have found favour with God, to be filled with the grace – the supernatural life – of God. It is to possess the Kingdom by belonging to the King (cf. *Mt* 5:3, 10).

As Mother of the King of kings, Mary bore the Kingdom within her. As Mother of the Messiah, she is also the Mother of the Church. Pope John Paul II wrote that "in her new motherhood in the Spirit, Mary embraces each and every one in the Church, and embraces each and every one through the Church."[26]

Mary and Elizabeth, bearing their sons – one a prophet, the other the Son of God – prefigure the Church that would later be born from the side of the crucified Lord and made manifest on Pentecost (cf. *CCC* 766, 1076). Blessed by the Father, impregnated by the power of the Holy Spirit, and filled with the Son, the Virgin brings joy and gladness into the dark, silent womb of man's deepest longing.

Like St Augustine, John Paul II provided a profound reflection on the belief and faith of Mary. He wrote:

> In the expression "Blessed is she who believed", we can therefore rightly find a kind of "key" which unlocks for us the innermost reality of Mary, whom the angel hailed as "full of grace". If as "full of grace" she has been eternally present in the mystery of Christ, through faith she became a sharer in that mystery in every extension of her earthly journey.[27]

The miracle of Mary's pregnancy and Virgin birth go hand in hand with the mystery of faith.

---

[26] *Redemptoris Mater* (1987), 47.

[27] *Ibid*. 19.

At Christmas we celebrate the birth of the Christ child while recognising that Christ always remains in the heart of Mary. Having given birth to the Saviour at one particular moment in time, Mary has continued to give the Saviour to the world ever since. It is her one desire, her unending gift of joy and life to each of us. "And how does this happen to me", we ask ourselves, "that the Mother of my Lord should come to me?"

# Solemnity of the Nativity of the Lord (Christmas)

Readings: *Is* 52:7-10; *Heb* 1:1-6; *Jn* 1:1-18

*"There has fallen on earth for a token*
*A god too great for the sky.*
*He has burst out of all things and broken*
*The bounds of eternity:*
*Into time and the terminal land…"*[28]

In those opening lines of his poem, "Gloria in Profundis", G.K. Chesterton provides a small but brilliant glimpse into the great mystery of the Incarnation and the joyful feast of Christmas.

How, really, can such a marvellous truth be expressed fully? Actually, it cannot be expressed fully, and that is part of the wonder of it all: the indescribable and all-powerful Creator dared and designed and deigned to become man. "And the Word became flesh", wrote St John in the great Prologue to his Gospel, "and made his dwelling among us, and we saw his glory as of the Father's only Son, full of grace and truth."

---

[28] G.K. Chesterton, "Gloria in Profundis" (1927).

The many readings for the Christmas liturgies – the Vigil Mass, Mass during the night, Mass at dawn, and Mass during the day – present a glorious mosaic bursting with prophecies uttered and fulfilled, genealogies recounted and realised, proclamations issued and received, and love poured forth and embraced in faith both quiet and ecstatic. Throughout, there is a constant movement from God towards man and, in response, man towards God: a circle of direct communication flowing from the gift of divine communion.

God always initiates; he proclaims words of promise – "your saviour comes!" (*Is* 62:11) – and he shines a great light into the darkness of human history. The Virgin Mary, we hear, "was found to be with child from the Holy Spirit" (*Mt* 1:18). God breached the walls of the world through the faithful *fiat* and welcoming womb of the sinless Jewish maiden. And this without the fearful shouts that accompanied the emperors, but with joyful, angelic exclamation. "He has", wrote Chesterton, "strayed like a thief or a lover" into the wild places of the world and the human heart.

The readings make mention repeatedly of God's proclamation, appearing, coming and speaking – and of his doing so in definitive, earth-shattering terms. The opening chapter of the epistle to the Hebrews states, "Long ago, at many times and in many ways, God spoke to our fathers by the prophets, but in these last days he has spoken to us by his son." (*Heb* 1:1-2). In John's Gospel, the entrance of the creative Word into creation is described as light shining into darkness, just as light broke into darkness at creation: "The true light, which gives light to everyone, was coming into the world" (*Jn* 1:9; cf. *Gn* 1:3-5).

When light meets darkness, there is division. The world rejects the light because it claims to be above such division; in reality, the world rejects the definite lines and clear shape of the Incarnate Word, who scandalises with his particularity – born of a first-century Jewish girl in Bethlehem! – and with his perfect power: "He was in the beginning with God. All things were made through him" (*Jn* 1:2-3).

This divine paradox has always been a source of consternation to those who do not accept Christ; it has always been a source of joyful consolation for those who accept him. Some of this delight in the incalculable wonder of the Christmas mystery is conveyed in an Eastern Christian hymn:

> He has come down to us from a mother all-pure and yet he has remained unchanged: he has remained true God as he was before, and has taken on himself what he had not been, becoming Man out of his love for man.

So, what is the point of Christmas? That is, why did God become man? The *Catechism of the Catholic Church*, in one of its most unsettling and glorious paragraphs, quotes

St Irenaeus: "For this is why the Word became man, and the Son of God became the Son of man: so that man, by entering into communion with the Word and thus receiving divine sonship, might become a son of God" (*CCC* 460).

The Son has come so that we might become sons; a "god too great for the sky" dwells among us. Merry Christmas!

# PART TWO

# ADVENT AND
# THE HAIL MARY

This booklet is a companion to another CTS publication: *Praying the Our Father in Lent*. In that booklet I explored how the words of the "Our Father" can shape our Lenten preparations for Easter in a profound and fruitful way. In this booklet, I offer an exegesis of another beloved prayer of our Tradition, the "Hail Mary". This is a prayer that many Catholics pray every day, some of us many times a day, either on its own or in the course of praying the Holy Rosary. The following thoughts are intended to help make this beautiful and glorious prayer a part of your own journey towards Christmas, a means of preparing your heart to welcome the Infant Christ.

# Mary's Gift of Self Points the Way

*"Hail Mary, full of grace, the Lord is with thee…"*

An *advent* is a coming; it literally means "to come to". The season of Advent anticipates the coming – or comings – of the Son: in his Incarnation two thousand years ago, in his future return in glory, and in the mystery of the sacraments, especially the Holy Eucharist. The *Catechism of the Catholic Church* states:

> When the Church celebrates the *liturgy of Advent* each year, she makes present this ancient expectancy of the Messiah, for by sharing in the long preparation for the Saviour's first coming, the faithful renew their ardent desire for his second coming. (*CCC* 524)

So Advent is ultimately concerned with the Son's coming in glory, when he shall "judge the living and the dead".

## The Coming of Mary's Son and Saviour

This might sound a bit unusual. After all, isn't Advent about preparing for Christmas? And isn't Christmas about celebrating the birth of the baby Jesus? It is, of course, but there are other questions to ask: Why was that baby born in a manger twenty centuries ago? Why is he coming again – as a grown and glorified King – and what does this mean for us? Are we more comfortable with a babe in a manger than with a conquering King? What is our place in all of these events?

Pondering our place in salvation history brings us to the feet of Mary, the Mother of the Saviour. Introducing *Redemptoris Mater,* Pope John Paul II writes:

> The Mother of the Redeemer has a precise place in the plan of salvation, for "when the time had fully come, God sent forth his Son, born of woman, born under the law, to redeem those who were under the law, so that we might receive adoption as sons. And because you are sons, God has sent the Spirit of his Son into our hearts, crying, 'Abba! Father!'" (*Ga* 4:4-6)

Here, in a nutshell, is the essence of Advent. God initiates; Mary responds. God offers; mankind receives. This is the way of love and faith.

As the sinless, holy Mother of God, Mary is a unique creature. But her perfection and holiness do not make her aloof or inaccessible. Instead, the Mother of the Saviour is a mother for everyone. She draws us near, desiring to reveal the fullness of her Son to the Church and to the entire world. It is fitting, then, that these reflections on the four weeks of Advent will draw upon the "Hail Mary" (dividing it into four parts) in contemplating the past, present and future advents of the Lord Jesus Christ.

Mary is the perfect example of one who is prepared for the coming of God. Young, poor and unassuming, she would become, by her free choice, the Mother of God. Faithful to God's promise, she embraced the first advent of her Son before it occurred. John Paul II describes Mary as:

> the one who in the "night" of the Advent expectation began to shine like a true "Morning Star"... For just as this star, together with the "dawn", precedes the rising of the sun, so Mary from the time of her Immaculate Conception preceded the coming of the Saviour, the rising of the "Sun of Justice" in the history of the human race.[29]

### Graceful Greeting for Grace-filled Lady

The simple words of the "Hail Mary" form a profound commentary on the coming of salvation, judgement, death, and eternal life. Formed from phrases found in Luke's Gospel and the ancient Tradition of the Church, the "Hail Mary" is like a snapshot taken of the Virgin from the perspective of heaven, then offered to those willing to consider the depths of its beauty and truth.

It begins with the words spoken at the Annunciation. The angel declared, "Hail, full of grace! The Lord is with you!" (*Lk* 1:28). In *Redemptoris Mater*, John Paul II begins his

---

[29] *Redemptoris Mater*, 3.

reflections on this marvellous remark by emphasising that the plan of salvation, which is a plan of grace beyond words, means God sent forth his Son, "born of woman...so that we might receive adoption as sons". This announcement by the angel introduces Mary into the mystery of Christ. She is blessed by God "in a special and exceptional degree", a reality recognised by her cousin Elizabeth, who calls her "blessed...among women" (*Lk* 1:42).

As the *Catechism* notes, "Full of grace, Mary is wholly given over to him who has come to dwell in her and whom she is about to give to the world" (*CCC* 2676). Mary's "Yes" to God articulates the complete gift of herself to the God of Israel. "The grace with which she is filled", John Paul observes, "is the presence of him who is the source of all grace." And Christmas is about the gift of that source, the greatest gift ever given. It is salvation in Christ through sharing in supernatural, Trinitarian life.

Put another way, it means coming into intimate, life-transforming communion with God, the Source of all that is good, true and holy. It's the same communion received in the Blessed Sacrament. It's the same Lord who will come in glory to judge the living and the dead.

### The Coming (Again) of the Incarnate One

The Annunciation – the announcement of grace and favour on the young maiden Mary – marks the first time that the reality of the Incarnation was made known. Mary is "full of

64

grace", the Holy Father writes, "because it is precisely in her that the Incarnation of the Word, the hypostatic union of the Son of God with human nature, is accomplished and fulfilled."[30] Because Mary gave herself to God, God gives himself to mankind. The Son of God became the Son of Man so that by grace we might become what he alone is by nature: a true son.

Imagine the awe and wonder that Mary felt as the angel addressed her as "full of grace". Advent is a time to contemplate and experience the same awesome, wondrous power in the coming of our Lord. It is a call to awaken, to look up, and to rejoice. In the words of St Paul: "the hour has come for you to awake from sleep. For salvation is nearer to us than when we first believed. The night is far gone; the day is at hand" (*Rm* 13:11-12a).

### Towards the Fulfilment of the Kingdom

Advent is a season of hope and preparation. For what? For the return of the Christ-child as Christ the triumphant King. Which is why the Gospel reading on the First Sunday of Advent is taken from the Olivet Discourse. In it Jesus talks about another advent, his coming in glory:

Therefore, stay awake, for you do not know on what day your Lord is coming. But know this: if the master of the house had known in what part of the night the thief

---

[30] *Redemptoris Mater*, 9.

was coming, he would have stayed awake and would not have let his house be broken into. Therefore, you also must be ready, for the Son of Man is coming at an hour you do not expect. (*Mt* 24:42-44)

During Advent there is a continual connection made between the first coming of the Son and his second coming. Yet the term "second coming" can be misleading, since the Son's return is really a completion and fulfilment of his birth two thousand years ago, not some unrelated and disconnected event. In his Advent reflection in 2001, John Paul II highlighted the continuity between the two comings, writing: "Christ is the Alpha and the Omega, the beginning and the end. Thanks to him, the history of humanity proceeds as a pilgrimage towards the fulfilment of the Kingdom which he inaugurated with his Incarnation and victory over sin and death." For this reason, he explained, "Advent is synonymous with hope: not the vain waiting for a faceless god, but concrete and certain trust in the return of him who has already visited us."

Catholics are sometimes reluctant to talk about the return of Christ. Perhaps they think the topic is the property of certain Evangelical Protestants whose focus on the "rapture" and Christ's return can seem obsessive and imbalanced. Advent provides the right balance by rooting the return of our Lord in the Incarnation. "At his first coming he was wrapped in swaddling clothes in a manger," wrote St Cyril of Jerusalem in the fourth century, adding that "at his second coming he will be robed in vestments of heavenly light". May hope, preparation, joy and light fill our hearts during Advent.

# The Perfect Faith of the Blessed Virgin

*"Blessed art thou among women and blessed*
*is the fruit of thy womb…"*

"Hail Mary, full of grace, the Lord is with thee!" Uttered by the heavenly messenger, Gabriel, to a Jewish maiden (*Lk* 1:28), these words, of course, make up the first phrase of the "Hail Mary". The second phrase of that great prayer come from an earthly creature, Elizabeth, the cousin of Mary, who exclaims: "Blessed are you among women and blessed is the fruit of your womb" (*Lk* 1:42). St Bede remarks that this is fitting since the two remarks show that Mary "should be honoured by angels and by men and why she should indeed be revered above all other women".

The reverence paid to Mary by Catholics and the Eastern Orthodox is bothersome to some Protestants (and even some Catholics!), who see in it undue attention given to a mere human. It is attention, they say, fitting to God alone. This is an unfortunate misunderstanding, and one that is sometimes made worse by the inability of Catholics to explain the place and meaning of Mary in Catholic doctrine and devotion. Advent provides an opportunity to more deeply contemplate Mary's life as she emerges so prominently on the stage of salvation history during this season of preparation and anticipation.

Monsignor Ronald Knox once observed that Advent and Christmas mark "a return to our origins". Having been given the incredible news by the angel, Mary makes a return of sorts to her own origins, travelling to visit her beloved cousin – likely the closest living relative she had. She journeyed three or four days to the "hill country, to a town in Judah" (*Lk* 1:39), filled with the joy of news that was undoubtedly still overwhelming and mysterious. Luke shows that those who are filled with the Holy Spirit are anxious to tell others about Christ. And in his description of Mary greeting Elizabeth, he makes a similar point: those filled with the Holy Spirit recognise their Saviour – even when they cannot see him. "And it came about that when Elizabeth heard Mary's greeting," the evangelist writes, "the baby leaped in her womb. And Elizabeth was filled with the Holy Spirit" (*Lk* 1:41). It is then that the older woman exclaims in wonder at the blessed state of her young cousin.

How blessed was Mary? It might seem a frivolous question considering that she carried the Incarnate Son in her womb. But in order to appreciate the reverence due to Mary, it should be noted that the phrase "blessed are you among women" is the Jewish way of saying: "You are the most blessed of women!" And why has Mary been chosen by the Most High to be the Mother of the Redeemer? Because of God's grace and her faithful response to it, a fact that Elizabeth, herself a woman of great faith, recognised: "And blessed is she who believed that there would be a fulfilment of what was spoken to her from the Lord" (*Lk* 1:45).

Reflecting on Mary's faith, the *Catechism* compares Mary to Abraham, who, because of his faith, became a blessing for all the nations of the earth. Mary, because of her faith, became the Mother of believers, through whom all nations of the earth receive him who is God's own blessing: Jesus, the "fruit of thy womb". (*CCC* 2676). This promise of salvation is also found in Psalm 72:17: "May his name be blessed for ever; as long as the sun his name shall remain. In him shall all the tribes of the earth be blessed; all the nations shall proclaim his happiness."

In the original covenant made with Abraham in Genesis 12, the nomadic Patriarch is told by God that he will be made a "great nation", that his name will be made great, and that he "shall be a blessing" to all the families of the earth. So what does it mean exactly to be blessed? The very first use of the word "bless" in Scripture is found in the creation account of the opening chapter of Genesis, which describes God looking upon the creatures of earth, blessing them, and declaring: "Be fruitful and multiply" (*Gn* 1:22). Then, after creating man, he blessed Adam and

70

Eve and said, "Be fruitful and multiply and fill the earth, and subdue it" (*Gn* 1:28).

Blessing, then, is intimately connected to the gift of life. In the Old Testament, blessings were connected with prosperity, progeny and promise. Blessings and curses were central to the great covenants made with Abraham, Moses and David. With Mary, the blessing also involves prosperity, progeny and promise – but uniquely so, for her Son encompasses all of those things and makes them available to all people for the remainder of time. "For I tell you that Christ became a servant to the circumcised to show God's truthfulness," St Paul tells the Christians in Rome, "to confirm the promises given to the patriarchs, and in order that the Gentiles might glorify God for his mercy." (*Rm* 15:8-9). The promises made to Abraham are fulfilled in Mary; the Advent of the Old Testament finds completion in the Son of the daughter of Sion.

The Second Vatican Council declared that:

This union of the Mother with the Son in the work of salvation is made manifest from the time of Christ's virginal conception up to his death it is shown first of all when Mary, arising in haste to go to visit Elizabeth, is greeted by her as blessed because of her belief in the promise of salvation and the precursor leaped with joy in the womb of his mother.[31]

---

[31] *Lumen Gentium*, 57.

Because of her perfect faith and co-operation with God's grace, Mary is Mother of God and "mother of men, particularly of the faithful".[32] Mary is revered because she faithfully said "Yes!" to God and gave birth to the God-man. She is loved because she is our mother and the first disciple of her Son, our Saviour.

During Advent all Catholics can emulate the example of Elizabeth, the cousin of Mary. Filled with the Holy Spirit, she anticipates her Saviour before ever seeing him. She worships her Lord, even when he is hidden in the womb. She reveres and embraces Mary, who brings salvation to her and to the entire world. She hears the "Magnificat" and rejoices as Mary sings, "For behold, from now on all generations will call me blessed" (*Lk* 1:48).

### John the Baptist Prepares the Way for Christ

The prophet Isaiah and the evangelist Luke both mention two realities that might not appear, at first glance, to have a direct connection to the Christmas story: repentance and judgement.

The prophet Isaiah, in foreseeing the coming of a new and powerful "root of Jesse", writes that this perfect king "shall strike the earth with the rod of his mouth, and with the breath of his lips he shall kill the wicked" (*Is* 11:1, 4). Likewise, John the Baptist, the cousin of the Christ, promises fire and destruction for those who do not repent

---

[32] *Ibid.* 54.

and acknowledge that Jesus is the Messiah, crying out: "He will baptise you with the Holy Spirit and fire. His winnowing fork is in his hand, to clear his threshing floor and gather the wheat into his barn, but the chaff he will burn with unquenchable fire" (*Lk* 3:16-17).

In his book *The Advent of Salvation: A Comparative Study of Non-Christian Religions and Christianity*, Jean Daniélou writes of how the coming of Christ is perpetual and for ever in nature, and that John the Baptist fills Advent: "He it is who hastens the coming of Christ by sending out his resounding call to repentance, to conversion; and the power of his call makes men ready for Christ to come to them."

These extracts from Isaiah and Luke's Gospel are striking reminders of the need to be prepared to meet Christ at Christmas. Advent is an ideal time for Confession, a season for conversion and renewal of mind, and a time to prepare the way for the Lord in our hearts as Christmas approaches. By dying to ourselves, we open the way for the birth of the Saviour. In the word of the *Catechism*: "By celebrating [John the Baptist's] birth and martyrdom, the Church unites herself to his desire: 'He must increase, but I must decrease'" (*CCC* 524).

## *Theotokos*: Everything that Mary Is

*"Holy Mary, Mother of God…"*

God has a mother and she was chosen before the beginning of time.

This is an amazing belief, one that is sometimes mocked and often misunderstood, and misrepresented, sometimes even by Catholics. Yet this truth is at the heart of Advent and Christmas – as well as at the heart of the entire Christian faith.

This belief is also captured in a short phrase in the "Hail Mary": "Holy Mary, Mother of God". They are just five simple words, but words bursting with mystery and meaning. They tell us many things about Mary and about the Triune God and his loving plan of salvation for mankind, in which Mary has such a significant place.

Mary is holy. To be holy is to be set apart, to be pure and to be filled with the life of God. The call to holiness, the *Catechism of the Catholic Church* states, is summarised in Jesus's words: "Be perfect, as your heavenly Father is perfect" (*Mt* 5:48; *CCC* 2013). Mary's holiness comes from the same source as the holiness that fills all who are baptised and are in a state of grace. But Mary's relationship with the Triune God is unique, as Luke makes evident in his description of Gabriel appearing to Mary: "And the angel answered and said to her, 'The Holy Spirit will come upon you, and the power of the Most High will overshadow you; therefore the child to be born will be called the holy Son of God'" (*Lk* 1:35).

Possessing perfect faith, itself a gift from God, Mary was overshadowed by God the Father, anointed by the Holy Spirit, and filled by the Son. She was chosen by God to bear the God-man, the One in whom the "whole fullness of deity" would dwell (*CCC* 484). Completely filled by God, she is completely holy. Chosen by God, she is saved. Called to share intimately and eternally in the life of her Son, she was, the *Catechism* explains, "redeemed from the moment of her conception" (*CCC* 49) and "preserved from the stain of original sin" (*CCC* 508).

The Pentateuch contains the account of how God chose a small, nondescript nomadic tribe, the Hebrews, to be his "holy people" for "his treasured possession out of all the peoples who are on the face of the earth" (*Dt* 7:6). Many years later, in the fullness of time, God chose a young Jewish woman from a place of little consequence to be the Mother of God. This, in turn, would result in the birth of the Church, which Peter describes as a "chosen race, a royal priesthood, a holy nation, a people for [God's] own possession" (*1 P* 2:9).

Mary, faithful and holy, is chosen so that others can also be chosen and made holy, transformed by her Son into the sons and daughters of God and joined to the Body of Christ. Mary "is the *Virgo fidelis*, the faithful virgin, who was never anything but faithful," writes Fr Jean Daniélou, "whose fidelity was the perfect answer to the fidelity of God; she was always entirely consecrated to the one true God."

It has been said many ways and in many places but bears repeating that "Mother of God" is the greatest and most sublime title that Mary can ever be given. It sums up all that she is, all that she does and all that she desires. The title of *Theotokos* ("God-bearer", or "Mother of God"), far from being some late addition to Church teaching, is rooted in Scripture and the Advent story. The *Catechism* explains that Mary was "called in the Gospels 'the Mother of Jesus'" and that she "is acclaimed by Elizabeth, at the prompting of the Spirit and even before the birth of her son, as 'the Mother of my Lord'" (*CCC* 495).

Mary, the Mother of God, is also the first disciple of her Son, the God-man. She is also the New Eve, whose obedience and gift of her entire being overturns the sin and rebellion of the first Eve. Her Son is the New Adam, who comes to give everlasting, supernatural life and heal the mortal wound inflicted by the sin of the first Adam (cf. *1 Co* 15:45).

The lives and the love of the New Adam and the New Eve fill the season of Advent. Mary quietly and patiently calls all men to Bethlehem to see and worship the Christ Child. Jesus waits for mankind to recognise him as Lord and Saviour. But he does not just wait for us; he comes to us. His coming, however, awaits completion, both in our individual lives and in the life of the world. Which is why James, in his epistle, writes "Be patient, therefore brothers, until the coming of the Lord... You also, be patient. Establish your hearts for the coming of the Lord is at hand" (*Jm* 5:7-10).

Fr Daniélou explains beautifully this paradox of Advent, of Jesus having come already and yet coming still:

> We live always during Advent, we are always waiting for the Messiah to come. He has come, but is not yet fully manifest. He is not fully manifest in each of our souls; He is not fully manifest in mankind as a whole; that is to say, that just as Christ was born according to the flesh in Bethlehem of Judea so must he be born according to the spirit in each of our souls.[33]

Although young, most probably poor, and faced with incredible challenges, Mary waited patiently on the promises and the coming of her Lord and Son. The *Catechism* says that because Mary:

---

[33] Jean Daniélou, *The Advent of Salvation: A Comparative Study of Non-Christian Religions and Christianity.*

gives us Jesus, her son, Mary is Mother of God and our mother; we can entrust all our cares and petitions to her: she prays for us as she prayed for herself: "Let it be to me according to your word." By entrusting ourselves to her prayer, we abandon ourselves to the will of God together with her: "Thy will be done." (*CCC* 2677)

That is indeed the perfect prayer, from the perfect woman and mother, for Advent: "Thy will be done."

## Immaculate Mary

The great Feast of the Immaculate Conception is situated to draw Catholics more deeply into the mystery of God's grace, Mary's faith and the plan of salvation. Although not formally defined as a doctrine of the Catholic Church until 1854, belief in Mary's sinlessness goes back to the earliest centuries of the Church and is rooted in Scripture, especially the first chapter of Luke's Gospel.

In the encyclical *Ineffabilis Deus* (1854), Pope Pius IX formally stated the doctrine of the Immaculate Conception:

The most Blessed Virgin Mary was, from the first moment of her conception, by a singular grace and privilege of almighty God and by virtue of the merits of Jesus Christ, Saviour of the human race, preserved immune from all stain of original sin.

Although the Eastern Orthodox recognise and celebrate Mary's sinlessness, many Protestants do not. Some, in fact, take great offence at this belief, insisting that it makes light of Jesus's life, death and resurrection, and that it implies that Mary is more than a creature, perhaps even equal to her Son.

But the Church makes very clear that Mary's Immaculate Conception is a gift from God. After all, Mary was "redeemed from the moment of her conception", making it difficult for her redemption to be her own work. And Pope Pius IX's definition strongly states that the Immaculate Conception was "by a singular grace and privilege of Almighty God" and by the work and merits of Mary's Son. Sadly, some Christians not only reject this truth, they even resort to saying that Mary was "not special" or "not worthy of praise" – even though Mary, inspired by the Holy Spirit, declared that "from now on all generations will call me blessed" (*Lk* 1:48).

John Cardinal Newman once noted that Catholic beliefs about Jesus and his Mother are intimately connected and cannot be torn apart from one another. "Catholics who have honoured the Mother, still worship the Son," he wrote, "while Protestants, who now have ceased to confess the Son, began…by scoffing at the Mother." It is a cautionary statement that all Christians, including Catholics, should take to heart during the Advent season.

# Holy Mary and the Death of Sin

*"Pray for us sinners now and at the hour of our death. Amen."*

The final words of the "Hail Mary" are filled with comfort, but also with a reminder of our mortality and the inevitable end to our earthly lives: "Pray for us sinners now and at the hour of our death. Amen."

This cry to the Blessed Mother might seem distant from – if not at odds with – the season of Advent and the rapidly approaching season of Christmas. What does Advent have to do with sin? What does Christmas have to do with death?

Quite a bit, actually. In fact, it is difficult to appreciate Advent and Christmas without squarely facing the dark realities of sin, death and human failing. After all, God became man in order to destroy the power of sin. The eternal Word took on flesh and dwelt among us in order to conquer death. The perfect Son became a slave so that sinful slaves might become perfected, adopted sons.

## The Knowledge of the Immaculate Conception

"But," it might be objected, "what does Mary really know about sin and death? Didn't she escape both?" It's true that because she was immaculately conceived – a gift of God's grace – Mary was saved from sin. But because she is full of grace and in perfect union with her Son, Mary is able to see with utter clarity the human condition and the effect sin has had on the world and on mankind.

She rejoiced in God her Saviour (*Lk* 1:47) because she knew what sin was, though she remained untouched by its stain. As she stood at the foot of the Cross she experienced the heart-wrenching pain of seeing her Son and Saviour die a death for the sins of the world (cf. *Lk* 2:35).

So it is fitting and comforting that the Mother of the Son of God prays for her sons and daughters at the hour of their deaths. The Mother of God, from whose faith and body the Redeemer was born, prays that men and women will have the faith to become true children of God, born of the Spirit. The woman who experienced the death of her Son prays that men and women will die to themselves so that they will live in Christ (cf. *Ga* 2:20).

Some theologians have suggested that the Immaculate Conception was a doctrine meant to awaken the modern world to the fact that human perfection and salvation cannot come from technology, science or ideology, but only from God's initiative, mercy and grace. Modern man denies that he is a sinner in need of salvation. Contrast that to St Paul, who exclaims that "the saying is trustworthy and deserving of all acceptance, that Christ came into the world to save sinners, of whom I am the foremost." (*1 Tm* 1:15).

The true disciple of Jesus Christ must admit his need and his inability to save himself. He is then invited to become a son of God by grace and through divine adoption. This is the incredible reality of deification – man sharing in the freely offered life of God. In the words of St Hilary of Poitiers, "Everything that happened to Christ lets us know that, after the bath of water, the Holy Spirit swoops down upon us from high heaven and that, adopted by the Father's voice, we become sons of God" (*CCC* 537).

As the Gospel of Matthew states, Jesus is Emmanuel – "God is with us" (*Mt* 1:23) – making it possible for man to be with God and have intimate communion with him. And so the promise of Advent culminates in the fulfilment of Christmas.

## The Logic of the Assumption

What about the Assumption, the belief that Mary, at the end of her life, was taken up to heaven: How can Mary relate to those whose bodies will become corrupt in the grave? This doctrine has ancient roots in the Church's Tradition, but many find it puzzling, or even needless.

But the Assumption, seen in the grand picture of salvation history, is a matter of divine logic. Since Mary was sinless and since she bore the perfect Incarnate Son of God, it follows that her body – the tabernacle that bore the God-man – would not suffer the corruption due to sin. She would instead be glorified, just as all those who are filled

82

with grace and who have "put on the Lord Jesus Christ" (*Rm* 13:14) will one day be glorified.

As theologian John Saward explains:

> The Assumption is an application of the Lord's teaching when he raised Lazarus: "I am the resurrection and the life; whoever believes in me though he die, yet shall he live, and everyone who lives and believes in me shall never die." (*Jn* 11:25f) No one lives more truly in Jesus than Mary: he is flesh of her flesh. No one believes in him with greater devotion: "Blessed is she who believed" (*Lk* 1:45). Thus the *Theotokos* is not detained by death and passes into glory.[34]

Mary is all about her Son and is always going about his business in heaven as she did on earth.

In his encyclical *Redemptoris Mater,* Pope John Paul II explains a clear, beautiful truth about the Assumption: "By the mystery of the Assumption into heaven there were definitively accomplished in Mary all the effects of the one mediation of Christ the Redeemer of the world and risen Lord". And here is the glorious, joyous truth of Advent: "If as Virgin and Mother she is singularly united with him in his first coming, so through her continued collaboration with him she will also be united with him in expectation of the second".[35]

---

[34] John Saward, *Redeemer in the Womb* (Ignatius Press, 1992), pp. 57-58.
[35] *Redemptoris Mater*, 41.

Mary has experienced every joy and pain imaginable. She clasped in wonder the newborn Christ in her weary arms. She held in sorrow the bloody body of that same Son, grown and violently killed. She stands in heaven and patiently waits for her sons and daughters to come home.

## Rejoicing in Salvation

The evangelist Matthew summarises the message of Christmas when he writes, in the first chapter of his Gospel: "For it is through the Holy Spirit that this child has been conceived in her. She will bear a son and you are to name him Jesus, because he will save his people from their sins." The Lord has come, is coming, and will come again. Advent anticipates, Christmas culminates, and man rejoices: "Glory to God in the highest, and on earth peace among those with whom he is pleased" (*Lk* 2:14).

## A Christmas Confession

Commenting upon the final words of the "Hail Mary", the *Catechism* reflects:

> We give ourselves over to her now, in the Today of our lives. And our trust broadens further, already at the present moment, to surrender "the hour of our death" wholly to her care. May she be there as she was at her son's death on the Cross. May she welcome us as our mother at the hour of our passing to lead us to her son, Jesus, in paradise. (*CCC* 2676)

No one knows the hour of their death. But it will come, just as Christ will come. Both are good reasons to examine our consciences and to go to Confession before Christmas. Even if we have many years left to live, Advent is the time to die: to ourselves, our pride, our selfishness and our fears.

Jesus wants to come and fill our hearts completely with his light and life. As children of God, we are "partakers of the divine nature" (*2 P* 1:4) – if we are in a state of grace. "The soul of the deified person is a spiritual Bethlehem," writes Saward:

> a house of the Bread of Life, a cave that shines with the light of "God's and Mary's Son" newborn… The fulfilment of our deification is in the eternal Christmas of heaven, when we hope at close hand to behold the begetting of the Son by the Father and the breathing forth of the Spirit by the Father and the Son.[36]

As Psalm 24 exclaims, "Let the Lord enter; he is the King of glory." Heaven comes to meet us, so let us prepare ourselves to enter heaven.

---

[36] John Saward, *Cradle of Redeeming Love: The Theology of the Christmas Mystery* (Ignatius Press, 2002).